The Drier The Brighter

JUDY KENDALL

Published by Cinnamon Press, Meirion House, Glan yr afon,
Tanygrisiau, Blaenau Ffestiniog, Gwynedd, LL41 3SU
www.cinnamonpress.com

ISBN 978-1-905614-14-1
British Library Cataloguing in Publication Data. A CIP record for this book can be obtained from the British Library

Designed and typeset in Palatino by Cinnamon Press
Cover design by Mike Fortune-Wood from original art-work supplied by Dreamstime.com

Acknowledgements

The teachings of the Buddha.
Philip Gross for his tactful and astute responses to many of the drafts of these poems.
Martin Randall for his unfailing energy, encouragement and inspiration.
Tracey Gutteridge for her feedback on the collection; Barbara Dordi, Galya Marakova, Mary Ann Mooradian, Siobhan Wall and Linda Yeaton for comments on individual poems; and George Kendall, Alex Lipinski, Eleanor Kercher, Geoff Caplan, Piers Messum, Dilanee and Amali Bunter and Sue Bartlett for providing a number of the images.
Versions of these poems were first printed in *Envoi, Equinox, Obsessed with Pipework* and *Presence*. 'Accidental Commitment' received first prize in the *Envoi* 2005 international poetry competition. 'Rain Vision' was very highly commended in the Norwich Writers' Circle 2006 open poetry competition. 'The Anchoress' appeared in the MADBRIGHTON 2005 exhibition.
Thanks to a much-valued collaboration with digital artist Steven Earnshaw, interactive and digital versions of a number of poems 'appear online in PROOF, the Sheffield Hallam University creative writing journal.
Steve Marshall has made a musical setting of 'Still life with quinces and lemons' for chorus and recorder orchestra.

Accidental Commitment

Because I left the door ajar,
a sparrow hopped inside to scour
the skirting board for fluff,
twigs, leaves, a scrap of cloth
with which to line the temporary nest
it planned to build itself
within this bare-walled, desolate
and, what I would have called
till now, most uninhabitable heart.

Contents

To S. N. Goenka
and his assistant teachers of Vipassana meditation
in the tradition of Sayagyi U Ba Khin

The Drier The Brighter

lost

, thick mist

we have been walking miles

surrounded by peat hags
surrounded by acid-whitened stones

you unearth your compass
still puffing

I hold a corner of the map
if you dropped dead, I wouldn't have a clue

a hawk flies past
it took him a few breaths from the bottom

we go off in another direction
to meet black peat circles surrounded by white

the mist finally lifts

the age-long ridge falls beneath us
gathered
into folds of silk

-wards

The snow falls thickly,
a strong wind moves
the white-fronted geese flying south,
grey wings out of cold,
calling in half song,
half bark.

An early moon, knife-edged,
shining indiscriminately,
cuts light on anyone.

The train takes me north,
scooping into the cold
air, sharp and clear,
where there is no sound,
not one –
the fields unravelling,
the trees running backwards
in my wake,
behind.

patched work

... disconnected morphemes floated past

it was perhaps the sixth day that we fished for them
storing our catch in shallow bowls
where they shone, transparent
kaleidoscopic

certainly the temperature shot down

was it at that point that the seamstress was asked
to line language with things?

her needle ran hither and thither
with no time to cut patterns
sewing whatever was nearest to hand

I can see her now
racing the cold

but who remembers the cracking as the ice advanced

the rising and falling of lights...?

Lateral Moraine

with thanks to Bill Manhire

'Men say also ... but I have not seen' – Sir John Mandeville

Antarctica –
                    where the weather is made
deep white, the empty home of penguins,
skua-gulls, elephant seals, bodies
preserved in plenty of ice
carved out at the ocean edge:
vestiges of past polar expeditions.

This is the land of the story of the seal
that crawls the wrong long way up the valley
till, deathly tired, it lifts its head
to gaze one last time upon the impassable glacier-cliff,
sighs the seal-equivalent of 'shit',
and, rolling its eyes to the sky,
expires.

Each walker tests the surface
with an ice axe. Records remain of tunnels
to the centre of the earth, a stray yeti, the odd
polar bear, The Thing, its remake, lost
Atlantis, lost races, lost....
in the hut of Scott,
a smell of pony.

The Reckless Sleeper

on Magritte's painting, with thanks to Matthew Sweeney

I lie, unmoving, above the top bunk, bony on the luggage rack.
They have given me
no bedding, no pillow, but I am plagued with things –
a mirror angles at me the reflection of the dark, and something like a
bird perches
on my shoulder, whispering in the language of the train:

go to
sleep go to
sleep goa to
sheep

That ribbon is not mine – it belongs to the lady in the bottom bunk.
goat sheep sheep
deep
What's it doing, dancing among my things?
leap
Deeper, in the shadows, apple-grey, hides the light of the conductor.
Perhaps I should blow it out? If I could
weep

into the dark,
enter inter
enter the black
inter en terre
inter the dark
en terre enfer
en terre the dark
black sack of
en fer en fer

keep

5 am

these cold skies
cheating the dawn,

these bits of tree,
blocks of houses too close to houses,
shrouded people, shrinking in the weather.

early darkness
the cold slamming down
unprotected heads

One Minute's

surface of a cup
Twinings

11/11
11.01 am

Imperial War Museum café
window view:

                                                  birch
                              leaves
                                        lawn

un-
blurred / disturbed

Pieces

We sit in the unmade garden
in mid-argument,

you on the cleaner chair,
left leg crossed, ankle resting on right knee,

me on the dirtier chair,
right leg crossed, ankle resting on left knee.

Who is doing the mirror?
Ah, here starts another argument.

You stir
from one buttock to the other

and out of your loose black shorts
I watch your legs extend

how they place themselves,
how they shift, settle –

jigsaw pieces:
it would take one click.

Spring Hijack

Mid-March.

On one of those grey February-ish mornings with the lamps still on
I drive out of town in search of green.

Even here the land is road-riddled.

Snow, disguised as cloud, hangs above the AA-recommended inn,
brooding over the roundabouts and the petrol pumps,

traffic on my trail.

Some time soon the air will fill up with white,
and all the grave country roads will turn to car-park.

Brightening the Guest Room

on Van Gogh's Sunflowers 1888

the background stands out
in almost unbearable
yellow, foregrounded
by withered petals
and halfway down
at the broadest part of the vase
also brown
lies "Vincent"
in shaky blue

Take The Best View

a child's bed
hard springs and short
shoved against the door jamb

faces the window-sill base line
of a frameless square of green
that flows lightly uphill
dipping in trees and bulging hedgerows
till it spills out onto a tiny clouded rill of sky

dawn

waking almost too late
for the tiny gold stitches of cloud
a bird flies from one aerial to the next

the sun rises from behind a roof
the room turns pale yellow
I hide behind a vase

Wheat

on Van Gogh's A Wheatfield, with Cypresses 1889

in frame
less than stable
bubbles of wheat tumble
to the blue hills rolling
on a treetop prickle of porcupine-
branches stood on end
by the windy gusts of bright sky
strokes on the green
wafting in
from the cypress
this picture could stain
wind fanning wheat into gold
flames somersault
over the clouds dark-lit
across the border

On a Walk

The lower gate is open, leaning on a stone
far from its post,
the water trough unfilled,
there is no horse.

Down in the valley at intervals the crows give out a softened caw,
over the rise the rally scramblers hum and roar,
a tiny plane whines through the sky
and, rushing along the backbone of the hill,
the occasional in and out of waves of car –
measured against the liquid clatter of a single horse's hooves.

Which ones reflect my song?

My tread sets off a pheasant, startling the quiet air and me:
its indignant rattling flight, its body like a bottle –
its rapid whirring wings a fly's,
while the skylark's continual commentary
breathes in song and
breathes it out.

The horse hooves are slowing, cease,
the rally race announcer trails away
behind the sound of baaing sheep,
the upper gate clangs shut.

This is the day…

after Wally Page

This is the day the skylark likes
& so do I
This is the day the blue sky peeps
through the greying clouds
& the sun climbs high

When the sheep have eaten to their fill
when the air is fresh and the wind is still
& my feet cry out to be in the hills
& the midges dance up the little brook's rill
& so do I

Larksong

his notes ring together
the heather pricks my face
greenness in heaven

Watching the Praying Mantis

poised in prayer
his eyes, on stalks, turning in all directions

'do you think he can see us?'

perched on the ledge
his bright pale green forelegs
antennae-washing

our world stops
his takes over

Plough's Progress

with thanks to Philip Gross

The tall ship ploughed the sea
the sea scored the ploughshare
the plough cut through the ocean
the ocean broke up the clod

the clod rowed over the blue
the blue crafted a spade
the spade blued into a skiff
the skiff shot over a sail

the sail cut through a harrow of soil
that the plough crumbled back into clods
as all the sea's waters poured over the rake
who sailed far off into the blue

three wishes

thoughts wish for fire-irons:
to stoke into fumes

words wish for sticks:
to break up the bones

the itch, for a plough:
to make the blood run

midway

caught between Christmas and the New Year
more than half of Brighton's older West Pier

the thin struts that lead from the landing form
have been smashed by the steps of a winter storm

the shore-line is studded with tripod stands
Palace Pier investors, rubbing their hands

wood from the half-collapsed pavilion sweeps
southwest down the coast to Portsmouth beach

the wrecked silhouette hovers midway between
the braced lightness of air, the greedy pull of the sea

Spring

I looked down into the shady side of the garden. Spring lifted its head briefly in the form of a bluebell, not those real bluebells in the *Flower Fairy* books but the raggedy versions with upturned ends to the petals and a kind of mauvish hue.

Over the wall was the road. The kerb of the pavement on the other side was decked with uncut grass. It was mid-morning and the stream of traffic had thinned a little, enough to allow a glimpse of bare tarmac. It was a grey-white dull day, the air heavy with the moisture of threatened rain.

The Top of the Hanger

above Steep, Petersfield

below, it's spring, clear green

up here, no mist, no wind
the trees grey-brown and bare

as the hill turns
a chimney pokes up
then roofs rise
stringing along a road

a lop-sided sign dances in brambles
chairs lean, upended, against the patio table
a horse watches from the back-field
and the poet's house, carefully hewn
from red brick and oak,
tilts on the edge

On I Tow

on i tow on no wot i no
av luv   vul va
yes i sey   yes i sey
may i av luv   vul va i yam
now on w no won   now on w no won
no way   yaw on

the verge

bright yellow daffodils
running down the bank
not quite falling

the stream

Above Steep

where the sweet-toothed Edward Thomas lived with his family

The ruined cottage is no longer there
and it's the wrong season for periwinkles
but nettles and sticky weed
crawl in and out of the forest
over moss-encrusted logs
decades old
up the big long-legged lane
dark and bog-ridden
towards the hanger –
an hour to the top
over slippery chalk

He must have spent much of every day
travelling, and she,
with her groceries: flour, sugar

May Hill sequence

1
Light Leaves

the leaves on the beech have just uncurled –
seasoned, they'll grow dark and sturdy
but for now the light passing through their surfaces
is a pale refreshing green
softening tree trunks, earth, grass, air
lifting spirits

11
Dandelion Vision

someone is having a barbecue
voices carry more than a mile over grassland

from the sunken road
the meadow rises to eye-level
its raggedy green, its crop of dandelion heads
solid and light as balls

dandelions

dragged from the lawns
turfed out of the cornfields

111
The Bulbs of May Hill

when the hill is planted with conifers
and they spread their pine needle carpet
it becomes too dark for the bulbs
who wait

it can take a generation
before the trees are culled for furniture
but the bulbs seem to know –
one touch of sun on the earth
and that spring they'll come up

this year they are on a roll
passing the baton like pros

colour

well-practised
after all those seasons below ground

white yellow blue yellow

the elite academy of snowdrops
make way for the daffodils
the bluebells race to the foxgloves

there's even a flash of orchid –
no flower is ever extinct –
and months later the purple white-stalked crocus
leafless

Scenes from Dr Bach's Flower Remedies

Beeches tumble down the hill,
straining to meet the elms
that stand apart.

Grass stalks tangle in tendrils of chicory.

It is quiet.
The rain begins.

Below, near Walnut Tree Cottage,
water trickles down willow leaves,
Edward straightens, aspen-tall, his face a quiver of sky.

He must be looking for water violets.
All spring he has trawled the hillside for flowers
slouching up as far as the ancient track...

on this side, where prickles, yellow petals, defy the hopelessness
of gorse;
on that side, where larches start towards the sky.

uprooted

through mud I go
dragging a whole field along
half on each boot
ploughing on

Treading the Cotswold Way

I have walked too far, from cross dyke
to the Ring and back,
my head muddied with concern
about other heads' concerns.
I turn widdershins
to trace with shaky memory
the long path home
past wild thyme, quaking grass,
Roman Snails, adders
to where three black figures
rise over the horizon: man, woman, dog,
and slip three times in mud, marking my black coat,
staining my gloves.

In the early morning, roe deer come.

Song to the rain

Rain, rain, fall away.
Don't come back another day.

Keep falling. Keep
the cracking of my heart
at bay.

Smooth my wrinkled edges
with your downpour.
Wet them. Stay.

Keep dryness from me,
staving off the day.

Towards a Study (Chawton)

Teashop, cottage, donkey carriage,
draped by the shadow of the manor house
and half a hill.

All round the garden (reduced)
cottage flowers grow like weeds.
A woman digs.

Up in the dining-room,
its door left creaking,
on a tiny table

laid with inkpot and quill,
now blotter-less,
light pours.

The Demands of Colour

after viewing Southall's Portrait of Artist's Mother 1902

Recalling mediaeval recipes, her son mixes egg yolk,
water and powder paint. The fast-drying tempera
leaves him little time to fill in her square, slightly wrinkled, face,
her tight black cap and the lacy frill he had designed.
Next to her in the permanent exhibition rooms hangs
a painting of his wife. They share expressions.
Aware of the tempera's properties, of time, they stare forward
in the warm dark gallery light. They do not smile or frown.
Only in the grey of their eyes has he let a little colour burn.
Outside, December rain slants off the scaffolding,
as if shying from *Earth from the air*'s
four-foot colour photographs that brazenly retell
the new millennium in the bright greens of an Argentine plantation,
in the incredible mounds of fish in Senegal.

View from a caravan

Earlier the leaves' greens were what
struck me, not the haws. It was raining then,
wings fluttering in a puddle –
a bird's laughter?

Tonight it's the haws that are looking lovely,
the leaves less green,
and the bird's bath has shrunk
inside its gravel shore line.

Fraught

I'm practising aerial irritation.

The air is rippling
from breath and thrown stones.

Each oscillation
pushes me further from the true.

Think *plumb-lines*, I tell myself,

about to
topple.

Flailing,

I set my focus
on the sharp
rope underfoot,
the stretched tautness
in my legs,
the heat that gasps out of my
drying

womb

and rushes up my trunk to fill my face,
the itch dancing to unheard music
on what was once my fontanelle,

and somehow
keep standing.

too much autumn
the reds are almost scorching now
a mouth brimming with leaves

Words to love

Listen, love

listen, love
looks aren't everything

flab under the taut string vest
sick sweet teeth

bones meeting

Don't

head buried, trying
for the heart, between the breasts,
missing by inches

Hold me lightly

hold me lightly love
there is no room

soon I shall burst from your arms
like a butterfly from a ruined chrysalis
like the guinea worm from the stomach of its host

how your whole life

how
yourwholelife
isrippeda
parthowyoucanno
longertrustany
onehowtheonlymin
dyouknowisyo
urshownote
venth
at

There Being Nothing

things
people I love
the way they disappear
(impermanence)
into the brickwork and

there being nothing I can do about it

After the Iliad

by the blue Aegean sea
the great bronze scion gates
among the swords and fieldmice
golden helmets, beds of human hair
the naked woman wept

Living with angels

Cold eagles of desire.

Even when they don their human gear,
folded wings, covered halos,
nothing hides those glinting eyes.

So hard to emulate,
terrifying.

Does the dust rub off?

Not a breath

What does it take?

A hand on my back,
lightly,
a voice in my head,
the barest shift in decision.

leaving.

not one stick of furniture
in the room.
in the heart,

no tears.

The Anchoress

The aim is to achieve
an existence as simple and bare
as a coffin;

decoration
is being slowly stripped
from the six surfaces: walls, floor, ceiling.

So far she is down to a worn piece of rug over a fraction of the floor,
an old blue strip of towel on the wall,
no mirror,

a stool, a sleeping mat,
writing materials, a holy book,
an oil-lamp, a blanket and a twig for cleaning teeth.

The daily bowl, for food or excrement,
is passed by the helper
through a cat-flap in the door.

The world communicates through two slits in the wall.
There is little visual contact.
She finds direct daylight blinding.

She doesn't know it yet,
but underneath the slits
someone has painted a mouth for smiling

at misfortune, her own
or others'.

absence of birdsong

notes towards a death poem

6.00 am: traffic starts to shake the tower

hand writes

upper body in shawl, lower in blanket
a clock ticks
blood whistles in ears

pause to pick nose

back curves to ache, creasing stomach
slight stiffness on left side of neck
emptying head

ah, quietness!

Building

Gaudi's instructions to an apprentice (unsaid)

Work stone till it flows,
till pillars tilt,
till ceilings drip,
till floors undulate.

Roll up marble. Twist it into columns of smoke,
plait it into balconies and pout their lips.
Crease roofs. Stud them with ventilators
sheathed as warriors riding the swell.

Ignore the city fathers standing aghast,
the sponsors refusing to move in.

Do not consult.

This is how my 'Pedrera' broke the grip on the streets, and why
the cathedral is still building a hundred years after
a tram ran me over to strike out
no body in a hospital ward.

Undeterred

He threw a brick through the window
I double-glazed it

He picked the lock and made off with the computer
I took the chance to upgrade both

He took the car
I took up walking

He used a jemmy to break down the door
And take my tools, my iron, the upgraded computer and my aunt's antique mirror

The insurance came visiting
I wore a suit

I bought more expensive tools, irons and computers
Though I could not buy back my aunt's antique mirror

The police have padlocked the door back on its frame
And I am having a new one made of hardest mahogany

Next time he will respect the thickness of the door
That, at least, will be impregnable

Even if he carves it out, complete with frame,
And empties the whole house

Poem As House

after Lorine Niedecker

the room expands like a lung
drawing the cold wind in

        light shifts
        from patterned furniture
        to wall

and out of the open window
dust billows

Dawn Frieze

How clean the lines in an early morning sky,

Against washed rose, orange cream.

Single birds fly south,
Tiny silhouettes,

But there is always a rogue winging north.

I watch from my window, naming the colours.

A slow streak of cloud twists diagonal from the earth,

Jagged as lightning,
Bold as a witch.

Rain Vision

for Martin

Turning a corner, I see you looking up into the trees.

'Listen,' you say. 'The parallel universe of birds.'

I stop, arrested by your eyes, your half-collapsed umbrella.

'You look so happy,' I say.

You gaze at me, smiling.

The rain, the rain.

The Drier The Brighter

The colours wear themselves out
whirling tree shapes to the ground –
the fir-shaped fir,
the oak-shaped oak,
backed by a sky relief,
fathers like sons,
thin long birches,
European elms,
acacia-shaped acacia,
the drier the brighter,
blind bright,
blinding the eyes,
down to the ground.

Further off, there's rattling –
faster, furious.

A woman,
gale-force wind,
a falling tree.

After paucity of rain, short winters, cold, a dullish sky:
the brilliance of celibacy.

Lines of topography

Behind, the hillfort rises and dips,
barely threaded with harebell.

Above, birds mob a buzzard.

Below, the grassed-over slope falls away, ribbed,
down to a Constable:
tiny cows in a meadow, bordering trees.

Everywhere:
lines of topography.

Not Something To Take Seriously

The world is blue and grey.

Everything reduced somehow
to edges.

Each to our bit
in these pooh stick wars.

I cut into the pantomime.
My part is so amusing.

Muffing the duff lines. Laughing
at the thin clean light in your eyes.

Oh the craziness of it all –
not to be taken seriously.

Travelling

Sheep, stiles, hedgerow, lane, rough
squares of field, grass, stone wall,
wire, discarded tufts of fleece.

Words tumble. Some of my jokes
don't crack. We pant
and talk of everyday. Soft landings.

Trees shrink. The grass gets shorter. Hill
folds up into craggy peak. Sun comes out and vanishes.
Wind beats us.

On top, the atmosphere
turns to milk –
smooth as the Pennines it flows.

I walk down to the edge of a wood
where a branch of tiny stiff green fir-cones
dips into a pool of blue bells.

'Look!' The others are too deep
in talk, but a chocolate brown lamb tears over
from its flock of white and grey.

Later, sitting silent in my room, watching the sky –
colour melt orange-blue:
things I never do.

unfamiliar

withdraw from love, set back your sights

, refrain from reaching for the heights:

ward off that swooping wing

from titillation to the blight

that comes from tasting

of too much delight

; instead let space

stay unfamiliar

for more

of less

is

.

S T I L L L I F E W I T H Q U I N C E S A N D L E M O N S
STILLLIFESTILLLIFESTILLLIFESTILLLIFESTILLLIFESTILLLIFESTILLLIF
DILLLIFESTILLLIFESTILLLIFESTILLLIFESTILLLIFESTILLLIFESTILLLIFB
NLLIFESTILLLIFESTILLLIFESTILLLIFESTILLLIFESTILLLIFESTILLLIFER
EIFESTILLLIFESTILLLIFESTILLLIFESTILLLIFESTILLLIFESTILLLIFESTIO
UINCESSTILL LIFE WITH QUINCES AND LEMONSSTILLLIW
TILLLIFEWITHQUINCESANDLEMONSLIFEWITHQUINCESAN
NWITHQUINCESANDLEMONSQUINCESAND
SLEMONSWITHQUINCESANDLEMO
ENDLEMONSSTILLLIFEWITHO
OOOOOOOOOOOORANGEEEEC
D B B B BROWN OCHRE ORANGE FAWN N N N H
EOOOOOOOOCHREEEEEEEEER
RFAWNSTILLLIFEWITHQUINCESANDLE
USORANGEOCHREFAWNSTILLLIFEWITHQU
TUINCESANDLEMONSSPILLFROMTHEPICTO
CLLIFEWITHQUINCESANDORANGEPEELFROMTHR
ISTILLLIFEWITHLEMONSANDPEELFROMTHECLOA
POTHTHEFRAMESPILLFROMTHEPEELTHECLOTHN
SPILL FROM THE PEEL THE CLOTH THE FRAME
IFASIFASIFASIFASIFASIFASIFASIFASIFASIFASIFASIFASIFASISIFASIFASIFASG
EASIFASIFASIFASIFASIFASIFASIFASIFASIFASIFASIFASIFASIFASIFASIFASIFE
HSIFASIFASIFASIFASIFASIFASIFASIFASIFASIFASIFASIFASIFASIFASIFASIFAS
TIFASIFASIFASIFASIFASIFASIFASIFASIFASIFASIFASIFASIFASIFASIFASIFASIF
ASIFASIFASIFASIFASIFASIFASIFASIFASIFASIFASIFASIFASIFASIFASIFASIFAF
FIFASIFASIFASIFASIFASIFASIFASIFASIFASIFASIFASIFASISIFASIFASIFASIFAA
IFASIFASIFASIFASIFASIFASIFASIFASIFASIFASIFASIFASISIFASIFASIFAFW
ASIFASIASIASIFAS IF THE PICTURE DOESNT ENDENDNDNDDDN
SSIFITDOESNTENDNEDNASIFASIFFITDOSETNEDNETNIFISADISNTENDNNNNNN
AASASASASSASASASASASASASSSSENDENDENDENDNDNDDNDNDNNNNNNN
E M A R F E H T H T O L C E H T L E E P E H T M O R F L L I P S